PL

102 THINGS TO DO WHILE YOU WAIT ON THE PHONE

WALLACE WILKINS, Ph.D.

Published by
Hara Publishing
P.O. Box 19732
Seattle, WA 98109

Copyright 1996 by Wallace Wilkins, Ph.D.
All rights reserved

ISBN: 1-883697-46-8
Library of Congress Number: 95-081421

No part of this book may be reproduced, stored in or introduced into a retrieval system, or transmitted, in any form or by any means (electronic, mechanical, photocopying, recording or otherwise) without the prior written permission of the publisher.

Editor: Cherie Tucker
Book and cover design: Warren Wilkins
Layout: Katherine Whitehall
Proofreader: Vicki McCown

DEDICATION

This book is dedicated to each of you who continually seeks new ways to convert wasted time into constructive activities, higher achievement, and better moods.

Best wishes for great success!

INTRODUCTION

FAMOUS LAST WORDS
(Just before you're put on hold)

"Thank you for calling. Please hold."

"I'll see if he's available. Would you mind holding for just a second?"

"She will be with you momentarily. Hold please."

"Oops, I have another call. Would you hold for a sec?"

"All of our representatives are busy helping other customers. You will be assisted by the next available representative."

"Your call is very important to us. An operator will be right with you."

These are the last words you hear just before you're put on hold—just before you are left alone, unsatisfied, isolated, wasting your time with no positive way to control your situation.

How often do you hear these words? How much time in your life do you spend on hold? Think of what you could accomplish if you harness just a fraction of that time for useful purposes. At least, it would be better if you made your waiting time go by faster—with less irritation.

The activities in this book are designed to occupy your mind while you wait for a live person. Each activity provides a light diversion. Many of these activities simply distract your attention from your impatient thoughts and frustrated feelings. Other tips direct your attention toward productive activities, rather than just waiting helplessly. These suggestions focus on your relationships, your career, your health and your personal advancement.

Keep this book near your telephone. Read a page whenever you wait on hold. You can participate in each activity with your telephone tucked between your head and your shoulder.

These activities do not require intense concentration. They will not make you forget why you made your call. You will be in a better, more positive disposition when a live person comes on the line to greet you.

By the way, if you think of other things to do while you wait on hold, I welcome your suggestions. Use the forms at the end of this book to mail your ideas. My address is:

Wallace Wilkins
505 West Roy, Suite 402
Seattle, WA 98119-3883

I will be happy to give you credit for your original tips in the next edition of *102 **More** Things To Do While You Wait On The Phone.*

"Your call will be answered in the order in which it was received. Do not hang up. Hanging up will just delay your call."

"Are you still holding? I'm sorry. I'll try that extension again."

102 THINGS TO DO WHILE YOU WAIT ON THE PHONE

102 THINGS TO DO

1

Recite the alphabet skipping every other letter.

WHILE YOU'RE ON HOLD

Figure out how you could build a shed, starting with the roof and constructing it downwards.

2

102 THINGS TO DO

WHILE YOU'RE ON HOLD

Inspect the clothes you are wearing to see if they need cleaning or pressing. Do your shoes need shining or repairing?

102 THINGS TO DO

4

Prioritize the items on your to-do list.

WHILE YOU'RE ON HOLD

Pretend that the United States of America was to reduce the number of states to only 45. Which states would you recommend that we exclude? What are the advantages of excluding each of the states that you recommend? What are the disadvantages of excluding each of those states?

5

6

Identify one thing that you can do to improve a relationship you have been neglecting. Resolve to do it.

102 THINGS TO DO

WHILE YOU'RE ON HOLD

Select something that you have been putting off. If somebody else besides you were to accomplish it, what would be the first step the other person would take to be effective? Plan to take that first, effective step yourself as soon as you get off the phone. When you do, you will be as effective as that other person would have been.

8

Figure out what genetic structure a moth would need in order to avoid flying into a flame. What causes it to fly into a flame? What would have to be different to prevent this behavior?

9

Think about a different arrangement for your office furniture to increase your efficiency at work.

WHILE YOU'RE ON HOLD

10

Do you have a living will? Ask around to find out what a living will is. Consider having one drawn up for yourself and for members of your family.

WHILE YOU'RE ON HOLD

Think about your interactions with your co-workers. You may be experiencing difficult relationships with some of them. Of all of these people, identify the one person whose personality is most similar to yours. Take time to reflect on this difficult person who is most similar to you. Knowing that you are somewhat similar in your personalities, how can you use this information to approach that person in a more productive manner?

102 THINGS TO DO

Do you remember the last time you had a physical exam or a dental check-up? Plan to make an appointment for your check-up, or make yourself a note to prompt you when the time comes.

13

Think of your favorite house or apartment when you were growing up. How many windows did that favorite residence have? In your imagination, walk through that residence. Count the total number of windows you encounter.

WHILE YOU'RE ON HOLD

14

102 THINGS TO DO

Pull out some unfinished work. Make a little progress on it.

15

Practice thoughts that are relaxing and quieting. Let alpha waves cross your brain.

WHILE YOU'RE ON HOLD

102 THINGS TO DO

Rub your forehead. Then massage the muscles around your temples.

16

17

Look out your window. Search for something that you haven't seen before—something that you have always passed over. Enjoy the surprise.

WHILE YOU'RE ON HOLD

102 THINGS TO DO

Imagine what your response to the previous item would have been if you were a person who had been reading a Braille version of this book.

19

Proofread that letter or document you have been working on.

WHILE YOU'RE ON HOLD

20

Take off your shoes. Massage the muscles of your left foot. Then massage your right foot. Thank the person who left you on hold for giving you the time for a foot-massage break.

102 THINGS TO DO

WHILE YOU'RE ON HOLD

21

Think of someone who would really enjoy receiving a surprise telephone call from you––someone whom you haven't called in a long time. Look up that person's telephone number. Plan to give that person a "just thinking of you" surprise call. Anticipate the pleasure that both of you will enjoy.

22

Rehearse your presentation for the person you are calling.

Time your pulse rate. Count the number of heartbeats you have in one minute. Record your pulse rate in the space below. You will be asked to compare it with another reading later. If your pulse rate today is higher or lower than usual, what is happening in your life that explains why it is higher or lower?

My Pulse Rate Today Is: _____ beats per minute.
Today's Date: _____

WHILE YOU'RE ON HOLD

102 THINGS TO DO

24

Close your eyes. Hear a piece of instrumental music being performed by your favorite orchestra or band.

25

Imagine what you would do if all of the animals and plants remained the same and you were the last human on earth. What would you do next? And after that?

Rearrange words these a construct to sentence meaningful. Then sequence a this with random create sentence normal.

List as many state capitals as you can before someone comes on the telephone. Then list the South American capitals.

WHILE YOU'RE ON HOLD

Put your files
back in your
filing cabinet.

28

102 THINGS TO DO

29

Check your armpits for odors, just to be sure. What about your breath? Other odors from your body?
Be sure you are not being observed by your co-workers as you go through this checklist. If needed, take some corrective action.

102 THINGS TO DO

30

Think about the sounds you hear as you fall asleep. When people are used to noise, why does silence keep them awake? Several large cities have converted their transportation systems from elevated trains to underground subways. When the transportation goes underground, there is much less noise. When this happens, the people who live near the unused, elevated tracks are kept awake by the new silence. Why is this?

Open a window.
If your window
does not open,
imagine what it
would be like if it
did open.

WHILE YOU'RE ON HOLD

32

Spell the letters of the alphabet according to their pronunciations. (The letter "m" is pronounced "em." The letter "c" is pronounced "see.") Rearrange the letters of the alphabet in alphabetical order according to how they are pronounced. Which letter is farthest away from its normal position in the alphabet?

102 THINGS TO DO

Identify unique ideas for what you can do while you're left on hold. To have your ideas considered for the next edition of *Please Hold: 102 **More** Things To Do While You Wait On The Phone*, use the forms at the end of this book.

33

WHILE YOU'RE ON HOLD

102 THINGS TO DO

Pull out what's on the bottom of your in-basket. Handle it or heave it.

Think of all the people who get along with you at work. Identify the one whose personality is most different from yours. Is there something you can do to get to know and understand that person a little better?

36

Look at your wrist. Notice where your arm hair starts and stops. Can you see how different your skin is in the areas with and without hair? What explains this skin difference?

Make a note to buy a hand-held electric massager. Buy it soon. Buy it today, so you can use it tomorrow when you are left on hold. Massaging your feet, your forehead, your shoulders and your lower back will turn your waiting periods into rejuvenation.

WHILE YOU'RE ON HOLD

Rub your belly with one hand while you pat the top of your head with the other. Remember back to when you first did this trick. How old were you? Who was with you at that time? What were the circumstances?

39

Think about what you would do if you woke up and found that someone had stuffed your room with brand new $100 bills. Imagine their smell, their texture. Imagine whom you would tell. Imagine how you would spend them.

WHILE YOU'RE ON HOLD

List as many American and foreign automobile makes and models as you can before someone comes on the telephone.

40

102 THINGS TO DO

41

WHILE YOU'RE ON HOLD

Think about what changes would take place if the equator shifted so that a new equator ran through the North Pole and South Pole? Where would the sun rise and set? What would happen to time zones? What other changes would take place?

42

102 THINGS TO DO

Take one of your rings off your finger. Notice how it feels when you put it on your other fingers. Or take your watch off and put it on the other wrist. Notice how different it feels in the new position.

Recall a few of your major lifetime successes and accomplishments. Were they recent, or did they occur some time ago? What would explain when and how they occurred?

WHILE YOU'RE ON HOLD

44

Touch your hand to your cheek. Which is cooler, your hand or your cheek? Which is warmer? Touch other parts of your body with your hand. Notice which is cooler and which is warmer. Make some guesses about why your hand is warmer or colder than other parts of your body.

WHILE YOU'RE ON HOLD

Unwind the telephone cord that has gotten knotted up over many months.

45

102 THINGS TO DO

Close your eyes. As you concentrate on the patterns of light on the inside of your eyelids, let a visual image form. Those images are called "lidflicks."

Pronounce your last name, your middle name, and your first name backwards in that order. Change the order.

47

WHILE YOU'RE ON HOLD

48

Think of a person who deserves special thanks from you. Make an entry in your appointment book to go thank that person.

49

WHILE YOU'RE ON HOLD

Figure out why the colors of leaves change. Why do some leaves turn orange while others turn yellow, maroon, or red in autumn?

Make a list of people who deserve a compliment from you. Your list can include people at work and at home. Keep your list with you until you have given your compliments to those deserving people. Use your list as a reminder to do it.

102 THINGS TO DO

50

WHILE YOU'RE ON HOLD

Reflect on the advantages you have from being employed by your current employer. A lot of people don't have those advantages.

Recite the alphabet backwards.

52

102 THINGS TO DO

53

WHILE YOU'RE ON HOLD

Name one thing that you would never want said about you ever again. What plans and progress have you made to prevent that from being said about you?

Look up the phone number of a cordless telephone dealer. Consider buying a cordless phone so you will be able to move around your office the next time you are left on hold.

55

WHILE YOU'RE ON HOLD

See if you can move the middle toe of one of your feet without moving any other toe.

102 THINGS TO DO

Read a few
pages of the
book or novel
you have.

56

57

Rub the
back of
your neck.

WHILE YOU'RE ON HOLD

Anticipate your dreams and goals for the future.

102 THINGS TO DO

58

Fold your hands, lacing your fingers. Notice whether your left little finger or your right little finger is on the bottom. Unfold your hands and refold them so that your other little finger is on the bottom. Notice how weird this feels. By the way, about half of the people fold their hands in the manner that feels weird to you.

102 THINGS TO DO

60

For a change of pace, plan to take a different route home tonight. What turn-offs will be different on your way home tonight?

61

Construct a palindrome that is longer than Anna, Otto, and tot. A palindrome is a word or sequence that is spelled the same backwards as it is spelled forwards. Like: A man, a plan, a canal, Panama.

WHILE YOU'RE ON HOLD

Listen to your inner voice as it speaks to you when you are on hold. Some people have difficulty identifying their inner voice. If you are not sure about your inner voice, it's the little voice that may have just said, "What inner voice?" or "I don't have an inner voice." Now that you have identified it, listen to it as it speaks to you. Instead of listening to aggravating, negative messages from your inner voice, switch and listen for upbeat messages.

WHILE YOU'RE ON HOLD

Figure out how the pyramids were built without modern engineering technology. Do you have any guesses?

Back up your computer.

102 THINGS TO DO

64

WHILE YOU'RE ON HOLD

Reminisce about the most enjoyable vacation you ever experienced. How old were you? Where was it? What did you do? What made it so enjoyable?

65

102 THINGS TO DO

Scratch that special spot. Scratch around it. (Be aware of observers!)

66

WHILE YOU'RE ON HOLD

Think about someone to whom you could give a little help today. Plan to do that after you get off the phone.

Imagine what kind of scarf, necktie, shirt, or blouse would go better with the rest of your clothes than the one you are wearing today. Make a note to go search for it.

WHILE YOU'RE ON HOLD

Take off your shoes. Put your shoes on the opposite feet. Notice how weird they feel. Try walking with your shoes on the opposite feet while you're on hold.

102 THINGS TO DO

69

Create a shopping list of things to pick up on your way home.

Imagine what a fly must feel like when it keeps bumping against a window pane. Have you ever felt like that at work? Have you ever felt like that in any of your relationships? What will you do differently next time?

WHILE YOU'RE ON HOLD

Figure out something you can do today to make one part of your world a little more peaceful. Please go do it.

WHILE YOU'RE ON HOLD

72

Imagine that you were to design a brand-new athletic uniform. Which four colors would you use to make it extremely inspirational to the athletes and attractive to the fans?

73

Imagine that you had to be confined to just one location for the rest of your life. If you could choose the place, where would it be? Which special people would you invite to accompany you?

74

Excluding roses, list as many flowers as you can before someone comes on the telephone.

WHILE YOU'RE ON HOLD

75

Pretend that the United States of America was to increase the number of states to 55. Which countries from around the world would you recommend for statehood? What are the advantages of including each of the countries you recommend? What are the disadvantages of including each of those countries?

102 THINGS TO DO

Etirw ruoy eman sdrawkcab gnisu eht dnah taht uoy t'nod yllamron esu.

Do some filing.

78

WHILE YOU'RE ON HOLD

Sharpen
your pencil.

102 THINGS TO DO

Without using a computer or calculator, figure out how many seconds there are in eight years, four thirty-day months, three weeks, six days, twenty-three hours, and twelve minutes.

Check your appointment book to make plans for your upcoming engagements.

WHILE YOU'RE ON HOLD

Think about someone who will enjoy receiving flowers from you. Make a note to buy some flowers on your way to see that person.

81

82

WHILE YOU'RE ON HOLD

Organize your desk top. Reorganize it to experiment with a new arrangement.

102 THINGS TO DO

Think of something you can do today to help your favorite candidate win the next election.

Recount the many things that have gone well during your day. Plan ways to celebrate them.

84

WHILE YOU'RE ON HOLD

Imagine that there is one thing you could do, one step you could take, to supercharge your career. What would this one step be? Go do it.

85

102 THINGS TO DO

WHILE YOU'RE ON HOLD

86

Think about where
you will be spending
your next weekend.

102 THINGS TO DO

Make a note to buy a stack of greeting cards. Keep them close by to write to friends or associates the next time you are left on hold.

88

Use the electric massager you bought if you followed the suggestion offered in #37. If you bought your massager at that time, you know that massaging your feet, your shoulders, or your lower back can turn your waiting periods into pleasure. If you did not buy a massager back then, go buy it now.

Count the number of things in this book that you can do when you're on hold. There are not exactly 102. Are there 101, 103, or some other number of tips? As you scan these pages for the correct answer, identify which specific number was omitted or duplicated. Hint: It was not #1 or #102. You can do this page by page, or perhaps you can identify a sure-fire shortcut to get the correct answer faster.

89

90

WHILE YOU'RE ON HOLD

Look out the window. Focus on the third thing that caught your attention. What was it about that item that attracted your attention?

91

Improve your filing system. Review where you place your most frequently used files. Put your most frequently used files, not your most important files, closest to you.

92

Think about what people would do if rain fell upward from puddles toward the clouds. How would we modify umbrellas and convertible cars? What other changes would we make to accommodate rain falling upward?

WHILE YOU'RE ON HOLD

93

Do you have a will for your heirs? Is it up-to-date? Review all of your close family members. Do you know if anyone does not have a will? Make a note to have yours completed or brought up-to-date. Encourage the members of your family to take care of this legal matter soon.

Think about your last meal. How could your last meal have been more healthful? Plan your future meals around that more healthful menu.

Answer this question: Why do people do so many things to undermine their success? Why do they move close to their goals and then do something to trip themselves up?

WHILE YOU'RE ON HOLD

Close your eyes. Identify your favorite singer. Hear your favorite song being sung by your favorite singer.

97

102 THINGS TO DO

Guess how the walls in your room are constructed. What is on the inside of your wall--in the space between the wall of your room and the wall of the room next to your room?

Time your pulse rate. Count the number of heartbeats you have in one minute. Record your pulse rate in the space below. Compare your pulse rate with your pulse rate that you recorded at #23. If your pulse rate is different than it was before, what has been happening in your life that explains the difference?

My Pulse Rate Today Is:
_____ beats perminute.
Today's Date:_____

Do an inventory of your desk supplies. Make a note to order the supplies that are running low.

WHILE YOU'RE ON HOLD

> Imagine that you were the last human being alive. Is there anything you would wish that you had done before everyone else vanished? Make a plan to do it soon.

101

102 THINGS TO DO

Think about what you would do if you won the lottery—even if you don't play the lottery.

WHILE YOU'RE ON HOLD

102

Hang up. Call back later. You can always exercise this choice.

Please send me ____ copy(ies) of *Please Hold: 102 Things To Do While You Wait On The Phone* ($6.95 each). Add $2.00 shipping and handling for the first book, $1.50 for each additional copy. Washington residents add 8.2% sales tax. For quantity discounts and to order by phone, call 1-800-468-1994. Satisfaction guaranteed.

You can also mail this form with your check or credit card information. My address is:

Wallace Wilkins
505 West Roy, Suite 402
Seattle, WA 98119-3883

Order Form

_____
Name

_____
Address

_____
City   State   Zip

_____
Daytime Phone

_____
Credit Card Number   o VISA o Mastercard

_____
Expiration Date

_____
Signature

_____
Name As It Appears On Card

Suggestion Form

Dear Dr. Wilkins: Here's what I think people can do while they're waiting on hold:

_____

_____

_____

_____

_____

Please print clearly and sign.

_____
Your Name

_____
Address

_____
City   State   Zip

_____
Signature

My signature above gives Wallace Wilkins permission to reproduce this suggestion in future publications. In full consideration, I shall be credited by my name and city if my suggestion is included.

Please mail or fax this form to Wallace Wilkins, 505 W. Roy, #402, Seattle, WA 98119-3883; fax 206-284-1943. Thank you for your suggestion.

Suggestion Form

Dear Dr. Wilkins: Here's what I think people can do while they're waiting on hold:

_____

_____

_____

_____

_____

Please print clearly and sign.

_____
Your Name

_____
Address

_____
City   State   Zip

_____
Signature

My signature above gives Wallace Wilkins permission to reproduce this suggestion in future publications. In full consideration, I shall be credited by my name and city if my suggestion is included.

Please mail or fax this form to Wallace Wilkins, 505 W. Roy, #402, Seattle, WA 98119-3883; fax 206-284-1943. Thank you for your suggestion.